ZELDA THE ZEBRA

To Nathan,
Enjoy the journey!

Mary Jo Nyssen

Dedication

I dedicate this book to all of my loving grandchildren who inspired me to write this book.
Megan, Elise, Brynlee, Jenna, Kindra, Madelyn, Sarah, Michael, Robert and my new granddaughter, Hannah.

Madelyn's artwork was my inspiration for Hanna the Hummingbird.

ISBN: 0615386431
ISBN 13: 9780615386430
LCCN: 2010909691
Printed by Createspace

Introduction to the reader of

"A Colorful Journey Through the Land of Talking Letters"

Many letters of the English alphabet have more than one sound. Children usually learn the letter names of the alphabet – ABC etc. at an early age, but don't always connect that the letters make different sounds within words. Only the vowels a, e, i, o, and u say their letter names (long vowel sounds) in words. Within words the consonants make a sound different than their letter names. The letter Y has one consonant sound, and two vowel sounds of the letter I. Teaching children to understand these concepts will help them to become better writers and readers.

In this book, the sound of the letter is color highlighted in each reading. **The short vowel sound will be green, including the short vowel i sound of the letter Y.** **The long vowel sound will be red, including the long vowel i sound of the** letter **Y**. **A third vowel sound will be brown.** The consonants **C, G,** and **S** have 2 sounds so **their first sound will be pink,** and **their second sound will be orange**. The rest of the consonants which have one sound will be highlighted either in **purple** or **blue**. Knowing these basic sounds and their rules will help a child spell and read many words. It must be remembered that there are sometimes exceptions to these basic rules.

   This book will only address the single letters **A** to **Z**. It will not include the sounds of letter combinations such as **ay, ea, sh, th, oa, ch, wh, aw, oi, ck, oo, ou** etc.

"Hi Boys and Girls!
Welcome to "A Colorful Journey Through the
Land of Talking Letters!"
We are the letters from A to Z.
Come with us on this amazing journey.
Listen to each and every sound
In a land where colorful stories abound.
As we greet you from far and near
Be sure your ears are open to hear."

"**A**hoy! My n**a**me is **A**!"
"I h**a**ve 3 sounds:
Short sound as in **a**pple,
Long sound (when I say my n**a**me) as in
angel,
Third sound as in **a**ll."

3

Aa (short sound)

Andy **a**nd his f**a**mily climb their l**a**dders **a**nd pick **a**pples in the **a**fternoon. Then they store the **a**pples in their **a**ttic.

Aa (long sound)

April b**a**kes her f**a**vorite **a**ngel food c**a**ke. When she t**a**kes it out of the oven, she m**a**kes her t**a**sty frosting and ices the heavenly **a**ngel food c**a**ke.

Aa (third sound as in **a**ll)

Alm**a** enjoys bouncing her b**a**ll,
Painting p**a**lm trees on her w**a**ll,
Eating **a**lmonds in the f**a**ll,
T**a**lking when her sisters c**a**ll.

"Happy **B**irthday! My name is B!"
"I have 1 sound as in **b**ike."

On her **b**irthday **b**eautiful **B**rynlee rides her **b**lue
bike to the park to watch the **b**utterflies flutter
in the **b**reeze and hear the
brown and yellow **b**um**b**le **b**ees **b**uzz.

"**C**ongratulations! My name is **C**!"
"I have 2 sounds: **Hard sound** as in **c**at,
Soft sound as in **c**ity (I always say '**sss**' when followed by e, i or y.)"

Cc (hard sound)

Elise **C**atherine loves her **c**uddly **c**alico **c**at, **C**leo.
Cleo is a **c**ourageous and
clever **c**at be**c**ause he **c**aught
the **c**rafty mouse hiding in Elise **C**atherine's **c**loset.

Cc (soft sound)

Cynthia lives in the **c**ity. For breakfast
Cynthia enjoys her **c**ereal, **c**innamon rolls,
citrus fruit and apple **c**ider.

"Goo**d** **D**ay! My name is D!"
"I have 1 soun**d** as in **d**inosaur."

During **D**ecember **D**onal**d** **d**elivers **d**elicious **d**oughnuts to the **d**andy **d**inosaur two **d**oors **d**own from **D**anny's **D**iner.

"Good **Ev**ening! My name is **E**!"
"I have 2 sounds:
Short sound as in **ele**phant,
Long sound (when I say my name) as in m**e**."

Ee (short sound)
Eddie had an **ele**phant named **E**dgar. **E**dgar b**e**gged
Eddie to l**e**t him g**e**t an **e**ducation.
Eddie said, "Y**e**s!" Now **E**dgar is an **e**xc**e**ll**e**nt **e**ditor.

Ee (long sound)
An **e**mu named **E**dith lived in **E**gypt.
One **e**vening sh**e** watched th**e** **e**clipse of th**e** moon
while sh**e** ate her d**e**licious p**e**cans.

"**F**antastic! My name is **F**"
"I have 1 sound as in **f**ish."

Flora is a **f**amous **F**rench **f**lamingo.
She loves to **f**east on the tiny **f**resh **f**ish
in the water beneath her **f**eet.
From her **f**unny webbed **f**eet to the tip of her beak
she stretches to a tall **f**ive **f**eet.

"**G**reetings! My name is **G**!"
"I have 2 sounds:
Hard sound as in **g**oose,
Soft sound as in **g**iant (I can say the sound '**j**' as in
giant only when followed by e, i, or y.)"

Gg (hard sound)
Grandpa **G**oose has **g**olden **g**ladiolas **g**rowing in his
garden. **G**abby **G**oose loves to pick the **g**ladiolas
and **g**ive them to her **G**randma **G**oose.

Gg (soft sound)

Geor**g**e is a **g**iant **g**iraffe.
He and his friend **G**ypsy
eat their **g**in**g**erbread cookies
on the steps of the **g**ym.

"**H**owdy, Partner! My name is **H**!"
"I **h**ave 1 sound as in **h**um."

Hanna the **H**ummingbird **h**overs
over **h**er **h**eavenly purple **h**olly**h**ocks.
As **h**er quick flapping wings **h**um,
she **h**appily sucks the nectar from each bloom.

"Impressive! My name is I!"
"I have 2 sounds:
Short sound as in is,
Long sound (when I say my name) as in ice."

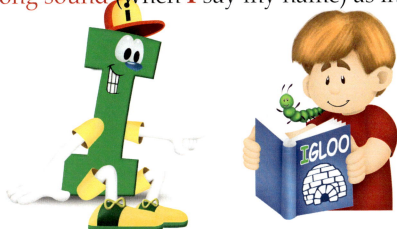

Ii (short sound)

Isidore lives with his inchworm, Izzy. They love
to sip on cold lemonade and read about igloos in
Alaska and penguins in Antarctica.

Ii (long sound)

While Irene was reclining on her bed an idea came
to her mind. Irene said to herself, "I shall plant irises
and eat ice cream all of my life."

"Enjoy yourselves! My name is **J**"
"I have 1 sound as in **j**ump."

In **J**uly, **J**enna **j**umps for **j**oy
when she **j**oins her friend **J**asmine.
They swim in the pool and en**j**oy
eating a **j**umbo **j**ar of **j**iggley gelatin.

"Let's fly your **k**ite, **K**indra! My name is **K**!"
"I have 1 sound as in **k**ite."

In the **K**ingdom of **K**arin there lived **K**indra who
was a very **k**ind princess. The **K**ing gave **K**indra
a **k**ite and a **k**oala bear when she graduated from
Kindergarten.

(**K**arin means **k**ind-hearted in Scandinavian.)

"**L**et's p**l**ay b**l**ocks! My name is **L**!"
"I have 1 sound as in **l**ove."

Michae**l** **L**aurence **l**oves his b**l**ocks
and his **l**ovab**l**e **l**izard, **L**uke.
A**ll** day Michae**l** p**l**ays with his **l**izard and bui**l**ds
launchers for **l**arge space ships with his b**l**ocks.

"Good **M**orning! **M**y na**m**e is **M**!"
"I have 1 sound as in **m**iss."

In **M**ississippi **M**adelyn and **M**egan sit under
a **m**agnificent **M**agnolia Tree in the **m**iddle
of the **m**eadow. They enjoy the sounds of the
Mockingbirds **mim**icking the calls of other birds.

(The **M**ockingbird gets its na**m**e because it **mim**ics
the sounds of other birds. It is the state bird for
Mississippi and
the **M**agnolia Tree is the state tree.)

"**N**ice to see you! My **n**ame is **N**!"
"I have 1 sou**n**d as i**n** **n**o."

Whe**n** **N**ed **n**oticed he had **n**o **n**oodles left to eat,
he we**nt** to the store.
Ned spe**nt** **nin**e dollars for more **n**utritious **n**oodles
a**n**d a **n**ewspaper to read while
he **n**ibbled o**n** his **n**ummy **n**oodles.

"Oscar is eating olives! My name is O!"
"I have 3 sounds:
Short sound as in on,
Long sound (when I say my name) as in old,
Third sound as in do."

Oo (short sound)
Bob has an obstinate ostrich named Oscar. When
Bob offers olives to Oscar,
he listens and runs back to Bob.

Oo (long sound)
Olivia relaxes on the porch of her
old h**o**me on the beach.
She watches the waves r**o**ll
over and **o**ver in the **o**cean.

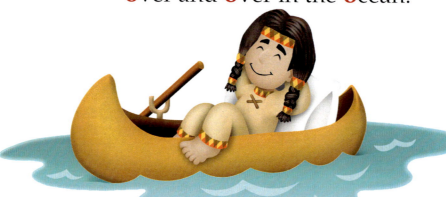

Oo (third sound as in d**o**)
Sam loves t**o** ride in his can**o**e.
At tw**o** o'clock what will he d**o**?
Go down t**o** the lake, and with no time t**o** l**o**se,
quickly he'll rem**o**ve his sh**o**es.
Then off he'll go in his can**o**e.

"**P**ardon me! My name is **P**!"
"I have 1 sound as in **p**enny."

Patty had an em**p**ty **p**ickle jar
full of **p**olished co**pp**er **p**ennies.
She **p**ut them in her **p**retty
pink and **p**ur**p**le **p**iggy bank.

"**Qu**iet please!" My name is **Q**!"
"In English words I am always followed
by the letter u."

Qu qu

"I have only 1 sound in English words,
'**kw**' as in **qu**een."

Queen's
Quarters

Queen **Qu**enna sat **qu**aintly sewing her **qu**ilt
while she shared her kum**qu**ats with her **qu**iet **qu**ail.

"**R**ock On! My name is **R**!"
"I have 1 sound as in **r**ock."

Robert rocks!

The **r**enowned **R**obert **r**eally **r**ocks when he plays
ragtime on his **r**egal saxophone.
At his **r**ecital he won a
red **r**ibbon for his **r**ocking **r**outine.

"**S**weet Dream**s**! My name i**s** **S**!"
"I have 2 **s**ound**s**:
The 'sss' sound as in **s**ang,
The 'zzz' sound a**s** in i**s** (My '**zzz**' sound i**s** never
u**s**ed at the beginning of a base word.)"

Ss ("**sss**" sound)
In the **S**outh of **S**pain **S**arah **s**kipped along the **s**ea
shore and **s**ang **s**weetly like the **s**kylark. She **s**ang
about a beautiful **s**enorita **s**tanding in the **s**and
beneath the **s**even **s**parkling **s**tar**s** in the night **s**ky.

Ss ("**zzz**" sound)

When Su**s**ie goe**s** to school she love**s** to
u**s**e her sci**ss**or**s** to cut out her letter**s**
and number**s**. She learn**s** to spell and
count and i**s** very wi**s**e.

"**T**errific! My name is **T**!"
"I have 1 sound as in **t**ur**t**le."

Tony has a **t**alen**t**ed pe**t** **t**ur**t**le named **T**ango who plays the **t**ambourine. **T**ango won a **t**rophy for his fas**t** **t**apping **t**une on his **t**ambourine.

"Cheer **U**p! My name is **U**!"
"I have 3 sounds:
Short sound as in **u**mbrella,
Long sound (when I say my name) as in **u**nicorn,
Third sound as in p**u**t."

Uu (short sound)

My **U**ncle **U**pton is an **u**mpire. One s**u**nny day when
it rained he stood **u**nder his **u**mbrella and **u**ttered
words of **u**nbelief as he looked **u**p to the sky.
"This is **u**tterly **u**nthinkable!"

Uu (long sound)
Ulanda the Unicorn, dressed in her frilly tutu,
used her unicycle and
played her ukulele in her stupendous universe.

Uu (third sound as in put)
Mister Bush, the butcher bought a pound
of sugar and a bag of apples
to put in his delicious sweet apple stew.

"Long li**v**e Italy! My name is **V**!"
"I have 1 sound as in **v**olcano."

Vincent took an ad**v**enturous **v**acation to Italy. He
made a **v**ideo of a **v**illage with **v**ineyards of grapes,
and the mighty **v**olcano, Mount **V**esu**v**ius.

"**W**elcome! My name is **W**!"
"I have 1 sound as in **w**ater."

William the **w**alrus made **w**arm **w**affles for breakfast
one **w**onderful **W**ednesday morning. He invited
the **w**ell-mannered **W**oodchuck to bring **w**edges of
watermelon for dessert.

"E**x**cuse me! My name is **X**!"
"I have 1 sound '**ks**' as in fo**x**."

Dressed in her e**x**quisite gown, Ma**x**ine the fancy
fo**x** and her friend, De**x**ter,
the very e**x**cellent ibe**x**, in his new tu**x**edo,
went to the e**x**citing party in their e**x**pensive ta**x**i.

"**Y**ippee! M**y** name is **Y**"
"I have 3 sounds.
In English words my first sound is my **consonant sound** as in **y**et.
I am used as a vowel to make the 2 i sounds:
Short sound of **i** as in g**y**m,
Long sound of **i** as in fl**y**."

Yy (consonant sound)
Yolanda the **y**ellow **y**ak lives in **Y**oko's back **y**ard.
All **y**ear she eats **y**ummy **y**ams
and plays with **Y**oko and her **y**o**y**o.

Yy (short sound of i)
At the school performance in the g**y**m, L**y**nn played the c**y**mbals, Cr**y**stal sang m**y**stical h**y**mns and D**y**lan recited l**y**rics from his book of poems.

Yy (long sound of i)
K**y**le's pig was in his st**y** when he saw a butterfl**y** in the sk**y** fl**y** b**y**.
The pig said "Oink!" and K**y**le said, "Oh m**y**!"

"Ama**z**ing! My name is **Z**!"
"I have 1 sound as in **z**oo."

Zelda the **Z**ebra always wears her cra**z**y sweater
with the silver **z**ipper. She lives in the **z**oo
and has an ama**z**ing garden of **z**innias and **z**ucchini.